MW01274468

The Music of
THE WORK AND THE GLORY

Volume 2

Music by
Lynn S. Lund

Lyrics by
Gerald N. Lund

BOOKCRAFT
Salt Lake City, Utah

Copyright © 1997 by Gerald N. Lund and Lynn S. Lund

All rights reserved. No part of this book may be reproduced in any form or
by any means without permission in writing from the publisher, Bookcraft,
Inc., 2405 W. Orton Circle, West Valley City, Utah 84119. Unauthorized
copying, arranging, adapting, or recording is an infringement of copyright.
The public performance of any of the works contained in this edition in a
dramatic form or context is expressly prohibited.

Bookcraft is a registered trademark of Bookcraft, Inc.

ISBN 1-57008-349-5

First Printing, 1997

Printed in the United States of America

Contents

GOIN' WEST 29
Chorus

Lyrics by Gerald N. Lund / Music by Lynn S. Lund

When it becomes clear that once again the Saints are going to be driven from their homes in beloved Nauvoo, Brigham Young gives the call for all to prepare to go to the Rocky Mountains. Soon the city becomes one vast workshop as preparations begin. Then, in February 1846, the great exodus gets under way, and the Mississippi River freezes solid enough to bear the weight of hundreds of wagons headed west. (Vol. 7, pp. 441–45, 625–31.)

I CAN'T WAIT TO SEE YOU 35
Mary Ann

Lyrics by Gerald N. Lund / Music by Lynn S. Lund

In a tragic accident Benjamin Steed gives his life trying to save his granddaughter. He is buried on the bluffs on the western banks of the Mississippi River. As Mary Ann prepares to start west, she stops at the grave to say one last good-bye to her beloved Benjamin. (Vol. 7, pp. 631–34.)

THE MORMON BATTALION 38
Men's Chorus

Lyrics by Gerald N. Lund / Music by Lynn S. Lund

While the Saints are still on the plains of Iowa, word comes to Brigham Young that war with Mexico has begun. When the government calls for five hundred volunteers from the Saints to march west in defense of their country, Brigham Young immediately responds positively. Within a few weeks, families are left behind, and one of the longest infantry marches in U.S. history begins. (Vol. 9.)

IN YOUR MIND AND IN YOUR HEART 43
Caroline

Lyrics by Gerald N. Lund / Music by Lynn S. Lund

As Joshua wrestles with spiritual things, not sure that there is a God who will answer him, Caroline seeks to teach him about how answers come. She explains that revelation usually comes to the mind or to the heart, and that when it does come it is often accompanied with a feeling of deep peace. (Vol. 8, pp. 435–39.)

LOVE MAKES A HOUSE A HOME 46
Women (Soloists and Chorus)

Lyrics by Gerald N. Lund / Music by Lynn S. Lund

When Brigham Young realizes that the Saints cannot make it to the Rocky Mountains in one season, he establishes Winter Quarters on the banks of the Missouri River. For months the Saints languish there in grimly inadequate shelters, in near famine conditions, and with only the most meager clothing. But this does not stop them from dreaming of their new home in the West. (Vol. 9.)

MAKE ME WHOLE 49
Joshua and Savannah

Lyrics by Gerald N. Lund / Music by Lynn S. Lund

After years of softening and being under his family's prayerful influence, Joshua Steed wrestles with the question of whether or not to ask of God if there is truth in what his family believes. When he hears his beloved Savannah put words to Olivia's song, he is touched enough to ask with a yearning heart. (Vol. 8, pp. 489–97.)

THE WORK AND THE GLORY FINALE 56
Chorus

Original lyrics by Gerald N. Lund; additional lyrics adapted by Gerald N. Lund from HISTORY OF THE CHURCH 4:540; W. W. Phelps / Music by Lynn S. Lund and from a Scottish folk song

In this final number, three themes from both of the albums are combined musically. "The Work and the Glory," "No Unhallowed Hand," and "Praise to the Man" all bear witness to the fact that it is God who is at the head of this work and who will bring about his purposes no matter what forces may oppose.

NO UNHALLOWED HAND

Joseph and Chorus

Original lyrics by GERALD N. LUND;
additional lyrics adapted by Gerald N. Lund
from *History of the Church* 4:540; W. W. PHELPS

LYNN S. LUND
SCOTTISH FOLK SONG

Driv-en from our homes in-to the win-ter night; Watch-ing flames con-sume all we own;

Hear-ing wid-ows weep, we see the or-phan's plight; Our hearts cry out, "O God, why is it

Copyright © 1997 by
GERALD N. LUND and LYNN S. LUND

4

5

No un-hal-lowed hand can stop the work of

No un-hal-lowed hand can stop the work of

God!

God!

ON THE PRAIRIE

Women (Soloists and Chorus)

GERALD N. LUND

LYNN S. LUND

Copyright © 1997 by
GERALD N. LUND and LYNN S. LUND

Fourth Soloist

safe - ty; Can - vas tents make up our cit - y On the prai - rie.

Chorus

Peo - ple are hud - dled near the fires,

Shiv - 'ring from the cold; And the blood of bare - foot

chil - dren Stains the prai - rie.

9

SEVENTEEN PEOPLE IN A ONE-ROOM CABIN

Benjamin, Mary Ann, Lydia, and Other Steed Family Members

GERALD N. LUND

LYNN S. LUND

Benjamin (verse 1)
Mary Ann (verse 2)

Sev - en - teen peo - ple in a one - room ca - bin, Wall - to-wall fam - 'ly just a-
Ev - ery-one's hun - gry, and we're all through eat - in'; Head - to-head bod - ies, so we

talk - in' and a - gab - bin'. Will we re - mem - ber all the fun that we're hav - in'
cer - tain - ly aren't sleep - in'. Nev - er com - plain a - bout the com - p'ny we're keep - in'.

When we find us a home?
Will we find us a home?

Copyright © 1997 by
GERALD N. LUND and LYNN S. LUND

14

15

ONLY GOD KNOWS HIS HEART

Benjamin and Joseph

GERALD N. LUND

LYNN S. LUND

Copyright © 1997 by
GERALD N. LUND and LYNN S. LUND

prom - is - es of change in each to - mor - row? For - give all that? Just
right have I to put a - side his griev - ing? I see it now, so

turn a - way? Ig - nore the wreck - age of his fool - ish choic - es? Who
clear and true! It's I who reaped the har - vest of my choic - es. My

rit.

makes it right? Who pays the price? Who stills the an - guish of the cry - ing
son is back, re - stored a - gain. The bit - ter - ness is gone; my heart re -

rit.

Joseph

voi - ces? On - ly
joic - es.

OLIVIA'S THEME

Instrumental

LYNN S. LUND

Copyright © 1997 by
GERALD N. LUND and LYNN S. LUND

A LEGACY OF LOVE

Women's Chorus

GERALD N. LUND

LYNN S. LUND

Ear - ly in the spring in Jo - seph's red brick store, The Proph - et spoke in coun - sel to the
"Char - i - ty is yours; it lies with - in your hearts. Com - pas - sion too is there in am - ple

sis - ters. "Now I turn the key for wom - en ev - ery - where. Go
meas - ure. Use these price - less gifts to lift and heal the world, And

This arrangement of "Legacy of Love" is available in separate sheet music in an SSA arrangement.
It can be purchased from Jackman Music, P.O. Box 1900, Orem, UT 84059. (801) 225-0859

Copyright © 1997 by
GERALD N. LUND and LYNN S. LUND

26

28

Lyrics:
We'll heal the wound-ed heart,

God. We'll heal the wound-ed heart, Of-fer com-fort to the wea-ry.

We'll cher-ish one an-oth-er, Watch o-ver one an-oth-er, With hearts knit to-geth-er in

love. With hearts knit to-geth-er

in love.

GOIN' WEST

Chorus

GERALD N. LUND

LYNN S. LUND

The black-smith's ham-mer is ring-in' on steel, Twist-in' i-ron un-til it squeals. The

Copyright © 1997 by
GERALD N. LUND and LYNN S. LUND

There's a place where we can rest. We'll find our moun-tain home And

call the land our own.

The

Is this our fi - nal test be - fore our work is done?

Some- where out in the West There's a place where we can rest. We'll find our

moun - tain home And call the land our own.

I CAN'T WAIT TO SEE YOU

Mary Ann

GERALD N. LUND

LYNN S. LUND

Copyright © 1997 by
GERALD N. LUND and LYNN S. LUND

leave.
tune;

I know you live, but still I grieve.
How sweet the times when we com - muned!

rit.

But soon I'll come, And we'll be one. I can't wait to see you when we're home.
Now you are gone, And I'm a - lone. I can't wait to see you when we're home.

rit. *mf*

1.

2. *mp*

If I could not fore-see the grand e-ter-ni-ties, Then I would feel an ev-er-pre-sent

p

THE MORMON BATTALION

Men's Chorus

GERALD N. LUND

LYNN S. LUND

Mor- mon Bat- tal- ion has been called to serve As sol - diers in a war with Mex - i - co. Our

proph - et de - cid - ed that we'll heed the call. We'll vol - un - teer and go where we must go. The

Copyright © 1997 by
GERALD N. LUND and LYNN S. LUND

Mor-mon Bat-tal-ion will re-spond with faith; We'll leave our wives and chil-dren for a time. ___ The

Lord will be with us if we're true to him And al-ways keep his pur-pos-es in mind.

We'll blaze a road where no trail marks the way; And we'll see the sun-set up - on dis-tant shores. The

way will be hot and the road will be long, But if we are stead-fast our glo-ry is sure.

The

Mor-mon Bat-tal-ion will re-spond with faith; And we'll leave our wives and chil-dren for a

41

42

IN YOUR MIND AND IN YOUR HEART

Caroline

GERALD N. LUND

LYNN S. LUND

turn now to God / And are hon-est in heart, / He'll give you the an-swers you seek. / Oh, doubt not the Lord; / He a-waits to re-spond / To those who are meek.

none else save God / Who can know all your thoughts. / He knows the in-tents of your heart. / In-qui-re of him; / He'll en-light-en your mind / If you do your part.

If you

Copyright © 1997 by
GERALD N. LUND and LYNN S. LUND

In your mind and in your heart, That is how his voice im - parts, All the
Cast your mind up - on that night When you cried out for the light, That you

knowl - edge your heart now de - sires. Let God speak un - to your soul, Till your
might know the truth of these things. God spoke peace un - to your soul, And you

heart and mind are full. What great - er wit - ness can you have_____ Than from
felt your heart con - soled. What great - er wit - ness can you have_____ Than from

1.

God?_____ There is

LOVE MAKES A HOUSE A HOME

Women (Soloists and Chorus)

GERALD N. LUND

LYNN S. LUND

We have

left our homes; Nau - voo lies far be - hind us. There we were rich - ly
find our home, a place which God has cho - sen. And when our jour - ney's

blessed. When the spring thaw comes, we'll find a place of safe - ty, A
done, Though our dreams are grand, it won't take much to please us, A

Copyright © 1997 by
GERALD N. LUND and LYNN S. LUND

48

Where an oak tree grows, And a large sun - ny kitch - en all
From a dry goods store. But I won't need a man - sion with

1.
filled with chi - na dish - es___ To re - mind me of home. Soon we'll

2.
all the fan - cy trim - mings; It's love that makes a house a home. It's

rit.
love that makes a house a home.___

MAKE ME WHOLE

Joshua and Savannah

GERALD N. LUND

LYNN S. LUND

Copyright © 1997 by
GERALD N. LUND and LYNN S. LUND

50

Bro - ken heart and con - trite soul? So much more to make me whole.

Who could ev - er heal this end - less pain?

mf

Now I think of those dark days And how my an - ger raged; I wound-ed ten - der hearts.

Al - ways quick to play the fool By break-ing all the rules, I lost the bet - ter part.

51

Long a-go I lost con-trol. Now I fear I've

lost my soul. How can I then hope for mer-cy from thee

now?

Savannah

Lis-ten to your heart, It will help you see

54

Joshua

Now, dear God, I cry to thee, Please hear and an-swer me, And tell me you are there.

I have wait-ed for so long To turn my life from wrong, Can I still find your care?

It's like I'm on fire with-in, Filled with light in

place of sin. Hope, like gen-tle rain, re-stores my soul. Cleans-ing power from Christ a-bove, Wit-ness of God's per-fect love; He has heard my cries and made me whole.

THE WORK AND THE GLORY FINALE

Chorus

Original lyrics by GERALD N. LUND;
additional lyrics adapted by Gerald N. Lund
from *History of the Church* 4:540; W. W. PHELPS

LYNN S. LUND
SCOTTISH FOLK SONG

Great is God's work and great is his glo-ry. He works to save and re-

Copyright © 1997 by
GERALD N. LUND and LYNN S. LUND

58

grow to fill the earth Till it pen - e- trates each land And the great Je - ho- vah's work is done.

grow un - til it fills the earth And— Je - ho- vah's work is done.

No un - hal - lowed hand can stop the work of God; The stand - ard of truth has been e -

Great is God's work and great is his glo - ry. He works to save and re -

rect - ed; It will grow to fill the earth Till it pen - e- trates each land And the

deem all men. He seeks full joy for all his chil - dren,

great Je - ho - vah's work is done.

To bring them home a - gain.

No un - hal - lowed hand can stop the work of God; The stan - dard of truth has been e -

Praise to the man_ who com - muned with Je - ho - vah! Je - sus a - noint - ed that

rect - ed; It will grow to fill the earth Till it pen - e - trates each land And the

Proph - et and Seer. Bless - ed to o - pen the last dis - pen - sa - tion,

60